MW00881303

The Real Life Sherlock Holmes

A Biography of Joseph Bell

The True Inspiration of Sherlock Holmes and the Pioneer of Forensic Science

**ABSO|UTE
CR|ME**

By Wallace Edwards

Absolute Crime Books

www.absolutecrime.com

Cover Image © Jason Stitt - Fotolia.com

Table of Contents

About Us

Absolute Crime publishes only the best true crime literature. Our focus is on the crimes that you've probably never heard of, but you are fascinated to read more about. With each engaging and gripping story, we try to let readers relive moments in history that some people have tried to forget.

Remember, our books are not meant for the faint at heart. We don't hold back—if a crime is bloody, we let the words splatter across the page so you can experience the crime in the most horrifying way!

If you enjoy this book, please visit our homepage to see other books we offer; if you have any feedback, we'd love to hear from you!

Introduction

When you think of Sherlock Holmes, you mainly think of a lanky aristocratic detective, smoking a pipe, draped in an Inverness cape and wearing a deerstalker cap, with his trusty magnifying glass in hand. While Sir Arthur Conan Doyle's beloved sleuth was known to use logic and forensic science in solving mysteries, there's much more to the story behind the inspiration of Sherlock Holmes. Doyle himself attributes his creation of Holmes to Doctor Joseph Bell, a celebrated forensic pathologist, physician and professor of medicine, revered for his unique skills at observation and deduction, whom Doyle once studied under when he toyed with the idea of becoming a doctor himself.

Chapter 1: Childhood and Education

Some would say Joseph Bell was destined to be a surgeon, as he certainly had science in his blood. He was the great-grandson of Benjamin Bell (1749-1806), considered one of the first major scientific surgeons. In fact, it was Benjamin Bell's six volume textbook, *A System of Surgery*, published in 1778 that helped set the standard for modern-day surgery. The book was widely popular and considered a Bible of surgical knowledge at the University of Edinburgh and other medical schools throughout Europe; by today's standards, the book is still referred to in some medical schools.

Joseph's great-grandfather was also noted for categorizing syphilis and gonorrhea as two completely separate diseases—a classification that would take the medical community decades to accept. A contributor in promoting wound healing, especially in terms of amputation, Benjamin Bell's *Theory and Management of Ulcers* (1778) is still considered one of the classic 18th century physiological texts.

This penchant for science and surgery would be handed down through many generations. Several of Bell's descendants, especially his son Joseph and his grandson Benjamin (Joseph's father) were also surgeons in Edinburgh. Like Joseph Bell himself, both of them eventually became president of the Royal College of Surgeons of Edinburgh.

Not much information exists about Joseph Bell's early life. He was born in Edinburgh on December 2, 1837 and raised in a deeply religious household. Much of Bell's religious faith would be inspired by his father's involvement with the Free Church, a Christian denomination with no government or state ties. Bell's father was adamant that young Joe be given a strict religious education and made a point of instructing him and his younger siblings on all things Biblical. A regular churchgoer, religion would clearly be an important factor for Bell throughout his life. Bell would continually refer to the Bible, both in terms of his personal life, as well as in his endeavors to help the less fortunate by donating to various charities throughout his career. He was also fascinated by nature, especially flowers and gardens, and was known to have had a penchant for planting and growing flowers as a young boy.

In 1843, Bell attended school for the first time at Mr. Macdonal's school. Unhappy with the education Joe was receiving, his parents transferred him to the Circus Place School in 1845 and then to Mr. Oliphant's school. At the age of 10, Bell entered the Edinburgh Academy, where remained until he was 17, studying such topics as Latin, Greek, French, German, Scripture, ancient history and English literature and criticism.

Bell's instructors at the Edinburgh Academy ranged from supportive to downright brutal. The Academy's math instructor, James Gloag, had a Dickensian reputation for being physically abusive to his students; he would beat them with a tawse (a leather strap with cut ends that resembled a cat o' nine tails). Quick-tempered and impatient with any pranks in his classroom, Gloag would often single out a student whom he felt was troublesome or interrupting his lessons and beat the child harshly. Back then this type of corporal punishment was rather commonplace; today, the teacher would be arrested for child abuse. While many students fell victim to Gloag's whippings, Bell escaped virtually unscathed, due largely to his studious habits.

Not all of Bell's experiences with teachers at The Academy were bad, however. Bell developed a strong bond with his Classics instructor, D'Arcy Wentworth Thompson. Far from the strict martinet that Gloag was, Thompson felt that whipping students did nothing to help encourage a student's education. Instead, he greatly respected his students, treating them as young adults, instead of young minds that didn't know any better. Thompson was so affected by the death of one of his students who had been falling behind in Latin, that he would go out of his way to help any of his students however he could. Bell appreciated and admired these characteristics, and would come to adopt them himself in later years, particularly in his work with children's welfare.

Bell was a good student and excelled in biblical scholarship, Greek, geography and math. Thin as he was (he's often remembered as a scrawny young boy with a wild mane of black hair), he was energetic and quite athletic. He often played the popular Scottish game of Hailes—a mix of shinty, which is similar to field hockey, and lacrosse. Bell was also a fine tennis player.

He also had a penchant for game hunting and spent much of his younger years in pursuit of critters, such as rabbits, hares, partridges and pheasants. In later years, Bell would become more of an observer rather than participant in sports, and his fascination would turn more towards the mechanics of boxing, cricket and football (soccer).

After completing his studies at Edinburgh Academy, Bell knew, like his ancestors before him, that he would enter the medical profession. The only question was where would he study? He debated at first whether to get his training in London or Paris, but in the end, the school that beckoned to him most was the University of Leyden in Holland.

At the time, the University of Leyden was one of Europe's most highly respected universities, home to such prestigious alumni as Philosopher René Descartes and US President John Quincy Adams. Bell's love affair with the school would not last long, however, as he soon found himself homesick, missing the comforts and familiarity of his hometown. Knowing that the University of Edinburgh had gradually developed a reputation as one of the top medical universities in Europe, he arranged for a transfer and chose to pursue his studies close to where he grew up.

The University of Edinburgh's progressive and philanthropic programs suited Bell well, and it's likely that his time there helped shape the direction he would later follow in his career. The university was home to the Royal Infirmary of Edinburgh, a teaching hospital, which offered students the ability to train and improve their medical know-how. The hospital also cared for destitute women, and students had the option to learn about midwifery and child care. The university's Public Lunatic Asylum was unique for its time, emphasizing the importance of treating patients with care and compassion, rather than mistreatment and neglect, which was what the mentally ill often received.

Aside from studying medicine, Bell also had a passing interest in literature, and dabbled in poetry throughout his life, his poems often revolving around nature and religious themes. He was extremely fond of the novels and poetry of his fellow Scotsman Sir Walter Scott, whose historical novels, such as *Ivanhoe* and *Rob Roy* are considered adventure classics, and the celebrated poet Robert Browning (*Bells and Pomegranates*). Both of these writers would greatly serve as a springboard for his future literary attempts.

As a medical student, Bell worked in the infirmary under Dr. James Syme as a dresser, or teacher's assistant, assisting Syme in surgical procedures, making sure the operating room was set up properly and managing the quality of surgical dressings. Syme was considered a medical pioneer in regards to his style of clinical teaching, which allowed for students to closely observe operations in the classroom. Syme grew very fond of Bell and the two developed a friendship that would last for decades. Bell adhered to Syme's philosophy that one must have complete knowledge of anatomy in order to perform surgery, which he would pass on to his own students in later years. Bell's tenure in Syme's medical wards would greatly influence not only his knowledge of surgical procedures, but help give him the confidence to perfect his own teaching style.

Bell graduated in 1859 from the University of Edinburgh at the age of 21. From this point on his career took off at a rather rapid rate. He was brought on to serve as Syme's medical assistant and house surgeon at the Royal Edinburgh Infirmary not long after he graduated. His thesis, "On Epithetical Cancer", received numerous accolades from the university's medical faculty. In turn, he was appointed Demonstrator of Anatomy at the university by professor John Goodsir, the university's chair of Anatomy. Bell would hold this position for two years, which was just the first step in a long and highly respected career.

Bell became a member of the Royal Medical Society of Edinburgh shortly after graduation in 1859. Throughout his life, Bell would write several textbooks and medical papers, the first of which was his monograph "Pulsating Tumour in Orbit Cured by Ligature of the Common Carotid", which was published in the Edinburgh Medical Journal in 1860.

In addition to Bell's love of gardens, he was also fascinated by architecture and home design. He wrote an article about different styles of homes that was published in *Cornhill Magazine* in 1860, a highly respected literary journal of the time, one that held novelist William Makepeace Thackeray as its editor. Bell's flirtation with architectural writing did not last long though, as this appears to be the only article of this kind that he ever wrote.

As Bell was embarking on his career in lecturing on surgery and pathology, as well as sowing the seeds of an interest in forensics that would eventually make him famous, he met Edith Erskine Murray, whom he courted and was engaged to in 1862. Edith was a beautiful woman, but it wasn't just her beauty that he found appealing though; like Bell, Edith was extremely kind-hearted. The two shared a devotion to religion, as well as many philanthropic tendencies.

Soon after meeting, the couple became inseparable. Whereas Bell was known to be quite gregarious, Edith was the opposite, her shy nature fading only with Bell and his family. Their engagement would last several years, as Joe was immersed in the start of his teaching career. They married on April 17, 1865. The couple would have three children: Jean, Cecilia and Benjamin.

Chapter 2: Career

It was during his courtship of Edith that Bell successfully passed his exam for the Fellowship of the Royal College of Surgeons in 1863. Dr. Syme encouraged the young professor to publish his graduate thesis, which he did in the *Edinburgh Medical Journal* that same year.

Having gone through years of medical school himself, Bell was often sympathetic to his students and encouraged them, very much in the same manner as D'Arcy Wentworth Thomas and James Syme both encouraged Bell. Bell required his students be punctual and alert at all times, yet he would go out of his way to show them kindness. Arthur Conan Doyle would fondly recall Bell's gregarious ways, especially in how he interacted with and supported the students; he considered Bell not just a professor or a mentor, but a personal friend.

Bell's career as an educator and house surgeon allowed him, through his lectures on operative surgery and laboratory courses, to demonstrate medical and surgical techniques, including the importance of surgical cleanliness and antiseptic applications.

The 1864 Diphtheria Outbreak

A crisis arose in 1864 when Edinburgh fell siege to a serious diphtheria epidemic. With unsanitary conditions being an issue, Edinburgh had fallen victim to many outbreaks over the years, including two cholera epidemics, typhus, typhoid and smallpox. Much of this was attributed to the city having open sewers, which were hot beds for bacteria.

Bell had been involved in assisting during the cholera outbreaks and sought to use his expertise to conquer this new epidemic. His efforts would be incredibly risky. While caring for children who had received tracheotomies during the outbreak, Bell was frustrated that there was no technology available to remove the infected membranes. He took it upon himself to experiment on a young child stricken by the disease. Since diphtheria affects the upper respiratory tract, Bell created a pipette (a long, glass tube) to suck out the bacteria from the back of the child's throat in order to help ease breathing.

It is not known whether the child recovered, but as a result, Bell himself was stricken with the disease. He left Edinburgh to recuperate for a period of three months. Although he eventually recovered from diphtheria, he did have some long-lasting effects, including the register of his voice being altered to a higher pitch and a stiffness in his legs, which affected how he walked for the remainder of his life.

Bell's Involvement with Nursing

One cause that was dear to Bell's heart was the need for proper nursing assistants. In the aftermath of the diphtheria epidemic, it would be crucial to have properly staffed hospitals, but in the mid 19th century, there were practically no nursing services available in England. Those that were available were positions mainly held by nuns and servants, who were improperly trained; many of them were mistreated and abused, and a large number of them were also alcoholics.

Taking the initiative, Bell began training nurses at the Infirmary in 1868. Prior to Bell's initiative, there wasn't much in the way of proper training available. Much of Bell's desire to instruct nurses was greatly inspired by Florence Nightingale's revision of the nursing system in England. She had revolutionized the overall scope of nursing during the Crimean War (1853-56), when she brought a staff of trained nurses to care for English soldiers at their base camp in the Crimea, now present day Ukraine.

Conditions at the camp were deplorable and bacterial infections were rampant. Nightingale and her team of trained staff helped save lives, even though poor nutrition and sewage issues were still a problem. Bell wrote to Nightingale for advice, following her establishment of the Nightingale Training School in 1860; she in turn encouraged and supported Bell in training prospective nurses, in a time when there was great need for additional help.

Bell not only sympathized with the limited number of nurses at the Infirmary, but it was his intention to properly train them and provide them with great respect in addition to looking after their welfare. Bell achieved great notoriety for his efforts and was instrumental in giving women a rare opportunity to involve themselves in the medical community, which would in the end help them find employment. Both Bell's and Nightingale's efforts helped revolutionize the nursing profession.

Modernizing the Surgical Theater

Bell clearly sought to bring surgery into the modern age. Bell applied carbolic spray (a type of antiseptic steam) in the operating room in an effort to help sanitize all equipment, as well as kill germs. Wearing the proper clothing during surgery was also a major issue of Bell's, as it could help prevent any type of airborne diseases.

As regular street clothes could be dirty and help spread bacteria, Bell was determined to curb this health risk. Keep in mind that during this time many operations were performed in unsanitary conditions; surgical gloves were several decades away, and many surgeons who wore gowns more than likely never changed them during the course of the day. Bell implemented the changing of clothes and, most importantly, the washing of hands to help combat the spread of any airborne diseases.

Forensics

Financial success didn't come easy for Bell. He struggled to maintain a consistent influx of students, while at the same attempting to set up his own private practice. And though his first book, *Manual of Operations of Surgery for the Use of Senior Students and Junior Practitioners*, received positive reviews when it was published in 1866, it wasn't enough to bring financial gain. Things, however, would turn around slowly in the years to come.

As a doctor, Bell supported preventive medicine, a progressive attitude at the time. Preventive medicine was important not just for curing disease, but in helping to prevent it by using proper forms of sanitation and modernizing sewage removal in an attempt to control diseases.

Bell's reputation was instrumental in his being appointed Assistant Surgeon to the Infirmary, as well as Examiner to the Royal College of Surgeons in 1869. He also developed a reputation for his medical articles, and in 1873, he became the editor of the *Edinburgh Medical Journal*, a position he held for 23 years until 1896. His position at the journal helped improve its quality by covering medical issues in other countries, as opposed to just Scotland, especially medical advances in the US. Despite his increasingly busy schedule, Bell not only wrote medical articles, but also provided reviews of all newly published medical books.

Yet Bell's fame could not prepare him for the tragedy that was about to strike, when his beloved wife Edith was affected with puerperal peritonitis, from which she died in 1874. Bell was devastated by Edith's death, and his black hair turned white literally overnight. In order to cope with this loss, Bell relied on his religious devotion for guidance, while also putting all of his energy into his medical research, and taking time to care for his children in the aftermath of her death.

Bell was clearly a devoted father and Edith's passing inevitably brought them closer together. His daughter Cecilia remembered how Bell would use his powers of observation and engage her and her siblings with a scenario that he referred to simply as The Game, in which he would observe other passengers and deduce not only where they were traveling to and from, but their occupations as well.

As Edith had been a source of stability and inspiration to him, he proceeded to follow up on a topic that they both cared about: providing care for the poor. As a result, Bell helped create the Longmore Hospital for Incurables in 1875, as a way to treat the poor and the homeless. Not only did he help establish the facility, he also heavily immersed himself in observing the status of the patients and made an effort to personally visit each and every one of them.

However, two important and relatively new fields of study, handwriting analysis and dialectology (the study of a person's accent and speech pattern), would greatly appeal to Bell and would have a positive impact on his life forever, leading him to become one of the leading figures in forensic science. A new science at the time, forensic pathology has since been used to determine medical jurisprudence, the cause of death, bullet trajectories, various diseases, fingerprinting, time of death and other issues. The ability to use new types of science as a tool to help solve crimes was one of Bell's passions.

In Scotland, medical jurisprudence was studied as far back as the early 1800s, but early forensics were very crude compared to the science we have today. Most criminal investigations relied on autopsies for hard evidence to determine the source of a crime. Autopsies allowed for further exploration of other issues related to a mysterious crime; there was enough medical know-how in the 19th century to study tissue samples, cells, organs and molecules, yet with such limited technology, it was still somewhat difficult to ascertain the cause of death.

The use of fingerprinting was just around the corner and DNA testing wasn't really used until the mid-1980s, so doctors in the late 19th century had little to work with. However, Bell was not one to be limited by a lack of technological advances, as he would soon prove with his involvement in several high profile murder cases.

Chapter 3: Introduction of the Method

Bell began to enlist the use of observation and deduction to diagnose his patients. Keen observations, he felt, allowed him another angle into medical diagnosis, and he was surprisingly accurate in his assessments. As time went on, these qualities would develop into a system, one that would eventually spawn one of the most cherished literary characters of our time. He called this system The Method.

Bell summed up The Method in just one sentence: "Observe carefully, deduce shrewdly, and confirm with evidence." It was a three part system that he followed religiously. In fact, he was so accurate in his observations that he could actually deduce qualities about individuals without ever asking them questions. This perplexed, awed and sometimes even soured his students, especially when he would turn his tests on them.

One time to see if his students were paying attention, Bell introduced a vial of brown liquid to his class, describing it as a potent drug. He decided to taste it by sticking his finger in the vial, tasting it and then making a sour face as if it tasted foul. He then passed it around to his class. The students all followed suit and were disgusted by the taste. Bell would laugh at their reactions claiming that they weren't paying attention, for although he dipped his index finger into the vial, it was his middle finger that he placed in his mouth.

Bell could determine a person's occupation simply by how they walked, or through their physical gestures. One famous encounter has Bell deducing that his patient was a cobbler because of a worn spot on the man's trousers just near the knee, as this was where the man would rest his lapstone, a piece of stone used in shoemaking.

Bell claimed that one should use their eyes and ears, as well as perception and powers of deduction, instead of one's hands to determine a person's ailments. He could determine what someone's profession was, if they smoked, if they drank, all by manner of acute observation.

The Method made Bell incredibly popular, and his classrooms were often filled to capacity. Students were in awe of Bell's power of intuition and his uncanny ability to deduce knowledge of his patients by just looking at them.

Another observation involved an elderly woman with a blister on her lower lip and a scar on her face. As she came before Bell, he asked her where her pipe was. She then produced a small clay pipe to Bell and asked one of the nurses to bring her to another room. As they were leading her away, she suddenly started to feel faint. Bell was able to deduce that the bruised lip and scarred cheek was actually a burn from the woman's pipe being lit too close to her face.

Bell could determine that another patient, without the patient uttering a sound, was from the Scottish town of Liberton, that he rode both gray and reddish-brown horses, and that he was employed at a brewery. How did Bell figure this out? He could deduce that it was Liberton by the specific type of mud on the man's boots, the horsehair was on his sleeves and as for the brewery, the man had a huge red nose.

The same went for a another patient, who arrived with a limp. Bell was able to determine that the man didn't suffer from hip problems, but instead suffered from severe corns on his feet, based on the pressure of the shoe against his foot. He could also detect that he was a serious alcoholic; he had a ruddy nose, his face was extremely bloated, his hands were shaking and his eyes were bloodshot...the dead giveaway was also the bottle of whisky in his coat pocket.

It was these very methods of observation that led to his involvement, at the request of the police, in helping to solve some of the most notorious crimes of the day.

One such case involved Eugene-Marie Chantrelle, a one-time medical student from France, who was accused of murdering his young wife, Elizabeth, whom he had seduced when she was just 15. Their relationship was extremely violent—he frequently abused her in a manner to exert control over her. Three months after taking out an insurance policy against her, Chantrelle discovered his wife unconscious from a coal gas leak in their home. He summoned Henry Littlejohn, Edinburgh's Police Surgeon, to investigate the situation. Being one of the first Commissioners of Sanitation and a lecturer for the Royal College of Surgeons of Edinburgh at Surgeons' Hall, Littlejohn and Bell were colleagues. And so Bell came along to inspect the situation as well.

When the two arrived, they found Elizabeth barely alive and transferred her to the Royal Infirmary, where she died shortly after. During her autopsy, Bell didn't detect any traces of coal gas. Since her organs would've reeked of it, he began to seriously doubt the plausibility of Chantrelle's story.

Bell then analyzed Elizabeth's pillowcase, which had a mysterious vomit stain. Vomiting wasn't indicative of coal gas poisoning, so he took the pillowcase to have it tested. After careful analysis, it proved to contain opium. Bell did a blood test and found that none of the substance had been injected, which led him to the conclusion that it had been ingested and that Chantrelle had poisoned his wife. He and Littlejohn discovered through their investigation that Chantrelle had recently bought large quantities of opium from a local pharmacy.

Though Chantrelle insisted he was innocent, there was no doubt that Elizabeth had been poisoned. Through research, Bell & Littlejohn also discovered a broken gas pipe in her bedroom. Bell located a plumber who had actually repaired the pipe a year before, further incriminating Chantrelle. The gas leak had been staged to give the impression that it was an accident. Chantrelle was convicted and executed for the murder in 1878.

Bell was later called upon to help solve the Jack the Ripper murders, which terrorized London in 1888. With the brutally vicious murders of five prostitutes, Scotland Yard again sought the expertise of both Bell and Littlejohn—the gruesome nature of the killings had led many to believe that the killer had surgical knowledge.

In addition to the murders, the anonymous killer had allegedly sent police investigators a series of letters, some of which have now been considered hoaxes, and Bell's forensic knowledge was used to analyze the handwriting. Both Bell and Littlejohn examined all elements of the case and were both surprised that they had chosen the same possible suspect, but they declined to make that information public: to this day the name of their potential suspect has never been revealed, though some believe both chose Montague Druitt, a local barrister, as their likely suspect. Druitt's father was a medical practitioner. It should be noted that within a week of sending their findings to the police, the murders suddenly stopped. It was also within a week that Montague Druitt committed suicide.

Bell became fascinated by the concept of the killer sending correspondence to the police. Not all of the handwriting matched, so it's possible that while some letters may be from the real killer, the others may be hoaxes. Over time, many suspects were removed from the list (there were at least 100 at one time) due to insufficient evidence. The identity of Jack the Ripper still remains a mystery today.

Chapter 4: Bell Becomes Sherlock

Doyle as a Student

Sir Arthur Conan Doyle first became acquainted with Joseph Bell in 1877, when he attended one of Bell's lectures as an 18-year-old student at the University of Edinburgh Medical School. Bell was actually one of Doyle's professors, and it was in 1878 that Doyle was brought on to serve as Bell's surgical dresser.

Doyle was greatly impressed by Bell's tenacity in the operating theater. Bell himself recollected how Doyle would take meticulous notes, transcribing Bell's lectures word for word, and occasionally asking Bell to repeat himself to verify that he had every word down. These notes of his would prove fruitful to him in the future, both as a potential doctor and as a writer.

Doyle was also observant of Bell's personality traits, taking note that Bell was especially kind to women and children, and that he had a sense of humor. Bell's wife Edith had once remarked that Bell could be quite entertaining in a deadpan manner, and that he employed sly humor when visiting with his patients, while also maintaining a serious side.

It was during this time that Doyle began to write stories. Aside from his medical pursuits, Doyle never stopped writing, but had limited success in getting his work published; several novels and short stories would be rejected. In fact, some of his works wouldn't be published until years after his death. Doyle counted among his literary influences his fellow Scotsmen, Sir Walter Scott and Robert Louis Stevenson, along with Edgar Allan Poe, Charles Dickens, and Wilkie Collins.

Many of Doyle's short pieces of fiction from this era were in the mystery genre, with his first successful venture into publishing being "The Mystery of Sasassa Valley," published in *Chambers's Edinburgh Journal* in 1879. Also in the same year, Doyle wrote a scientific article, "Gelsemium as a Poison," which was published in the *British Medical Journal*. The connection between Doyle and Bell would have its basis in medicine and literature.

Doyle's tenure as Bell's dresser gave him a great opportunity to get a full view of how forensics actually worked. Much of Bell's study focused on simple, basic movements, which allowed him to make a quick diagnosis that was primarily accurate. He had an uncanny ability to determine someone's occupation by the way they carried themselves as they walked. He was able to discern the differences between a sailor and a soldier for example. He could also deduce someone's occupation by looking at their hands. Also, having a keen ear, Bell could determine by accent alone where someone was from.

These keen observations of Bell's would come into play for Doyle, and he would use these methods of observation as the basis for one of his most celebrated literary characters, Sherlock Holmes.

As a student, Doyle would be employed as a doctor on a whaling ship (Hope of Peterhead) and then as a surgeon on the SS Mayumba on an excursion to West Africa in 1881. He would eventually finish his doctorate in 1885, with a thesis on tabes dorsalis, or the degeneration of sensory neurons.

Enter Sherlock Holmes

The world was first exposed to Sherlock Holmes with the publication of *A **Study in Scarlet*** in 1887. From the outset, you can see the influence of Bell on Holmes. The story chronicles the first meeting between Sherlock Holmes and his lifelong colleague, Dr. Watson. From the start, Holmes astounds Watson with his deductive capabilities; by shaking Watson's hand, he is immediately able to identify that Watson has had military experience. The mystery revolves around a dead body found in a Brixton tenement, with the word RACHE written in blood on the wall. After deducing that the victim was actually poisoned, Holmes takes notice of specific traits in the murderer, ranging from the type of boots he wears, the size of his feet, his height and even the kind of cigars he smokes. In the end it turns out that the murder is the result of a romantic liaison gone very wrong.

(There actually was a real Dr. Watson, who clearly inspired the fictional character. While a student at The University of Edinburgh, Doyle was acquainted with Dr. Patrick Watson, a colleague of Bell's, who was a highly respected surgeon and was known for his expertise in analyzing gunshot wounds. He was an expert on the subject of dietetics and nutrition, and he was appointed as personal Surgeon to the Queen).

Initially rejected by several publishers, the story originally appeared in *Beeton's Christmas Annual*, a popular magazine at the time. It finally appeared in book form in 1888, with illustrations by Doyle's father. The novel received a lukewarm reception at first, but grew in popularity over time. It was eventually published in the United States in 1890, and it has remained in print ever since.

Doyle was commissioned to write a sequel by Joseph Stoddart, the editor of *Lippincott's Monthly Magazine*, a well-known literary journal that published works by such authors as Willa Cather, Rudyard Kipling and Oscar Wilde, among others. *The Sign of the Four* appeared in 1890. While the story deals with a strange disappearance, mysterious treasure, and a secret, criminal pact between four convicts, the novel is famous for Holmes' rather explicit cocaine addiction, which he uses to help clear his mind. *The Sign of the Four* received a similar reception to *A Study in Scarlet,* yet the novel still remains popular for its complex plot and further insight into Holmes' character.

The Hound of the Baskervilles, in which Holmes and Watson attempt to solve a murder at a country estate where it is rumored that a fire-breathing hound lurks, is regarded as the most supernatural and macabre of the novels and appeared in 1902. The fourth novel, *The Valley of Fear,* appeared in 1915, and is considered by some to be the weakest of the novels, as it appears to recycle some plot devices from Doyle's short stories.

In addition to the four novels, Doyle would compose 56 short stories, which were actually more popular than the novels, all of which featured Holmes and his trusted assistant Dr. Watson.

Chapter 5: The Holmes and Bell Connection

While there has been much emphasis on the comparison between Bell and Holmes, it's probably impossible to determine where Bell begins and Holmes ends, since the two have been inextricably linked.

Doyle would claim in interviews that Bell was the inspiration for Sherlock Holmes. Both certainly have an expertise with forensics and deduction, yet whereas Bell is clearly a man of science, Holmes is also a superhero to some degree. Many of the characteristics attributed to Holmes were never at home in Bell, yet there are also a good deal of similarities the two share.

Doyle once stated that if Bell were a detective, he would more than likely be able to transform The Method into an exact science. Doyle also felt that Holmes, in his analysis of things, is deeply rooted in what he learned from Bell, and that he was clearly the literary embodiment of Bell, to which he graciously owed him a great debt for his inspiration in creating the character.

Holmes preceded many other famous fictional detectives and spies, such as Hercule Poirot, Miss Marple, Ellery Queen, Philip Marlowe and James Bond, minus all the gadgetry. But he's become perhaps the most famous of them all.

Holmes' meticulous devotion to his appearance and sometimes arrogant persona balances his ability for cunning logic in solving crimes.

Bell is described as keen-eyed and clean shaven with a ruddy face. Dr. Watson describes Holmes as over six feet tall, skinny with piercing eyes. Holmes also has a prominent chin and nose, as does Bell, while his hands are often smeared with ink and chemical traces.

While Bell enjoyed the occasional hunting expedition, he wasn't nearly as well-versed in weaponry as Holmes, who uses a variety of implements, such as a cane, a riding crop (Bell owned horses and a carriage, but it's not known if he ever used his riding crop in self-defense), fisticuffs and martial arts on occasion, as well as numerous pistols that would be used during various cases.

Holmes is, at times, portrayed as having an encyclopedic mind, in addition to being a highly cultured eccentric bohemian. He has an excessive knowledge of minutiae and is able to solve crimes that nobody else can. Yet much of this relates to both deductive and inductive reasoning, as well as using logic, observation and deduction as a means to draw a conclusion. He's also well-versed in a myriad of topics, including botany, geology, chemistry, anatomy and law, as well as being an expert violin player and speaking multiple languages, such as Latin and French.

While Holmes is an avid pipe and cigarette smoker, he also uses narcotics, such as cocaine and morphine throughout his life. He is also an oenophile, with a penchant for French wine. However, there is no evidence to suggest that Bell was a user of drugs at all. And given his devout religious background, it's highly unlikely. Bell was also against smoking; throughout his teaching career, he informed his students to avoid tobacco for its harmful consequences.

Bell's use of The Method clearly plays a part in Holmesian deductions. With inspiration from Bell, Doyle was able to incorporate his knowledge of forensic science, as well as his ability for deduction and apply it to the character of Holmes. Doyle also managed to give Holmes an air of sophistication which, in addition to his powers of deduction, more than likely made him incredibly appealing to readers.

Holmes is fascinated by science and chemistry. His interest in forensics no doubt plays a part in his characterization over time, as he analyzes a variety of objects, such as footprints, tobacco ashes, gunpowder residue, bullets, and even fingerprints, all of which helped set the stage for modern forensic investigations. Although all of this takes place nearly 100 years before DNA analysis become commonplace, the methods of deduction in Holmes' time could still be seen today as revolutionary, but crude. In fact, many of Holmes' uses of forensics would not even come into use until the turn of the century. Fingerprints, for example, would not be used fully to help solve cases by Scotland Yard until the early 1900s. Much of Holmes' scientific methods of deduction were seen at the time as pure fantasy. Yet it was through Holmes that these practices gained validity and eventually became implemented by detectives and scientists over time.

The Bell/Holmes connection didn't enter the public consciousness until after the publication of *The Sign of the Four*, the second Holmes novel, and the debate continues well into the present day as to how much of a connection there really was. As Sherlock Holmes became more popular over time, the press also became more intrigued by Doyle's elicit Bell/Holmes connection.

As Bell started to make a name for himself, he spoke openly about his friendship with Doyle, and initially seemed to somewhat enjoy the attention he gained from the Holmes character. Bell actually wrote an introduction to the 1892 edition of *A Study in Scarlet*, where he openly described his fascination with detective literature, while also praising Doyle and how, as a medical student, Doyle's attention to detail carried over into his fiction. Bell also remarked that Doyle was a natural storyteller, who has a unique ability to create realistic story lines and complex plots.

However, over time Bell grew more tired of the continuous comparison between himself and Sherlock Holmes, claiming in an interview from 1901 that the whole issue was silly, and that the whole thing was exaggerated, preferring to be known instead for his scientific and medical contributions. Many interviewers were equally fascinated by Bell's use of The Method, and his approach to using deductive reasoning.

Bell's daughter Cecilia made it clear that there was no connection between the two, stating that where Holmes appears brusque and stern, her father was actually gentle and warm-hearted. But to the young Doyle, writing the stories, and working as Joseph Bell's dresser as a medical student, this would be in line with his perception of Bell. Bell was more distant to him during that time, an approach that could've been viewed as slightly cold, again influencing his Holmes character.

Holmes and Forensic Science

Though Bell clearly was the pioneer of early forensics, it was Doyle, through Sherlock Holmes, who was actually responsible for forensic science becoming more widely known and accepted. At the time, few of his peers actually utilized Bell's practices, yet Holmes made it more readily acceptable to do so.

In the very first novel, *A Study in Scarlet*, Holmes discovers a new test that differentiates human blood from other fluids. The test for blood would actually help set the stage for future blood-related investigations. From the scientific background of both Bell and Doyle, for many budding chemists and scientists, Holmes' hemoglobin test was seen as a revelation, as it helped set the stage for the evolution of detecting blood in crime scenes, as well as testing blood overall. It should also be noted that *A Study in Scarlet* was published one year before the Jack the Ripper murders rocked London.

While he had chosen a career in literature over medicine, Doyle clearly had enough scientific know-how to create medical scenarios in his stories. Trace evidence, ballistics, toxicology and fingerprint analysis were all new when the Holmes novels and stories were written. Today, these are all used in major crime investigations. In fact, just watch any episode of "Law & Order", "The Mentalist", "CSI", or "NCIS" and you'll see deduction and modern day forensic science at work.

The use of forensics was so revolutionary that by the 1930s, Holmes' techniques had become part of traditional crime scene investigations. By the time Doyle passed away in 1930, scientists were able to determine mud samples and their origin, as well as the detection of stains, handwriting samples, and different types of dust. Footprints were also being used with greater frequency to deduce a crime scene, whereas today, all of these tests are par for the course.

Holmes on Stage and Screen

Sherlock Holmes remains a pop culture icon to this day. According to the Guinness Book of World Records, Holmes is the most portrayed character in the movies and has been portrayed by over 70 actors in a variety of theatrical, film and radio, comic book, board game, and video game adaptations of Doyle's novels and stories. The character's first appearance in the theater dates all the way back to a short play entitled *Under the Clock* in 1893.

It was American actor William Gillette, however, that first helped to define the image of Holmes that is forever ingrained in our minds, both by wearing the deerstalker cap and the now trademark calabash pipe. Gillette portrayed Holmes on stage from 1899 through 1930 and is also credited with using the phrase 'elementary' as a catchphrase, which gradually evolved into "Elementary, my dear Watson" over the years.

Gillette adapted elements from two of Doyle's stories, as well as *A Study in Scarlet*, with Doyle's blessing to create the play *Sherlock Holmes, or The Strange Case of Miss Faulkner* in 1899. The play toured throughout upstate New York and Pennsylvania before landing on Broadway, where it ran for seven months before embarking on a national tour, which was a tremendous success.

The first actual cinematic portrayal of Holmes occurred in 1900, in the film *Sherlock Holmes Baffled*. The 30-second film starred an unknown cast, and was actually considered a lost film for decades until it was rediscovered in the late 1960s.

Yet the two actors who will forever be associated with Sherlock Holmes are Basil Rathbone and Jeremy Brett.

Rathbone portrayed Holmes in 14 Hollywood films, from 1939 to 1946, all of which were wildly popular at the time. Rathbone definitely looks the part, as he clearly has the same angular features as Bell. The Rathbone-Holmes films are entertaining, but it's interesting to note that the first two films of the series are set in the proper Victorian era, while the remaining 12 are set in contemporary times, where Holmes, through his powers of deduction helps to thwart the Nazis.

Jeremy Brett appeared in the British anthology series, *The Adventures of Sherlock Holmes*, which consisted of 41 television adaptations of Doyle's stories, including the novels *The Sign of the Four* and *The Hound of the Baskervilles*, that were broadcast between 1984 and 1994. While not as well known as the Basil Rathbone films, many critics and fans claim that Brett's performance *is* the definitive portrayal of Holmes.

Brett apparently kept a huge file of notes, which allowed him to study every detail about Holmes, including mannerisms and the many quirks found throughout Doyle's stories; he often noted differences between the scripts and the original stories. In an interview, Brett claimed that Holmes was the hardest role that he ever played.

In addition to Gillette, Rathbone and Brett, Sherlock Holmes has been portrayed by a wide variety of actors, such as John Barrymore, Michael Caine, Peter Cushing, John Gielgud, Charlton Heston, Frank Langella, Christopher Lee, Roger Moore, Leonard Nimoy, Peter O'Toole, Christopher Plummer, George C. Scott, and most recently Robert Downey Jr.

Bell himself would get the rare television treatment by Ian Richardson in a series of films entitled *Murder Rooms: Mysteries of the Real Sherlock Holmes*. Unfortunately, the *Murder Rooms* films feature a wildly inaccurate portrayal of Bell, teaming him up with Doyle as a pair of caped crusaders, while using dramatic license to depict the similarities between Bell and Holmes. Aside from these exaggerations, the film series was extremely popular, but what's most interesting is that Richardson not only looks like Bell, he appears to embody his scientific spirit.

Holmes' long lasting scientific endeavors have been such a part of our culture that he was bestowed with an honorary fellowship by the Royal Society of Chemistry in Northern Ireland in 2010, the first fictional character to be so honored.

Chapter 6: Joseph Bell's Later life

Bell maintained a busy schedule in his later years. He continued with his medical and forensic work, but also gave in to other pursuits.

Still fascinated by sports, Bell become a member of the Lawn Tennis Club of Edinburgh. He eventually became a huge tennis fan; when not playing, Bell would analyze the game from a scientific perspective. Cricket, gardening, ornithology and hunting were still passions of his, and he was known to take down many a grouse during his shooting expeditions.

Such cheerful endeavors would be short lived as tragedy struck Bell again with the unexpected death of his son Benjamin in 1893 from peritonitis. His colleagues said the effects of his son's death clearly took a toll on him and that it seemed to age him greatly.

With barely two months to mourn the loss of his son, Bell was called upon by Scotland Yard for his assistance in the Alfred Monson case in 1893. Monson was hired in 1890 as a tutor for teenaged Cecil Hambrough, who came from a well-to-do family. The Hambrough family had leased the Ardlamont Estate for a hunting vacation in August of 1893. Monson accompanied the family and took Cecil fishing in a rowboat, which started to leak and eventually capsized. The two successfully made it to shore.

The following day Hambrough, Monson, and Edward Scott went on a hunting expedition. Hambrough and Monson were both carrying shotguns (Scott apparently had no weapon and would disappear into the unknown shortly thereafter). A shot rang out and when Monson and Scott returned to the mansion, they informed the staff that Hambrough had accidentally shot himself in the head, while attempting to climb over a fence. He claimed that all three of them had become separated during the hunt, when Monson heard a shotgun blast. Responding to the sound, they discovered Hambrough was dead.

It was then discovered that Monson had taken out a life insurance policy on the young Cecil Hambrough, from which he would inherit the equivalent of $1,000,000. Monson's reason for this, he explained, was that Cecil's mother had been advancing him large quantities of money against Cecil inheritance, and he wanted to insure Cecil in order to protect the advance.

It was initially accepted that Cecil's death was accidental. After some time had passed, Monson filed for the insurance claim, where he was informed that the claim was invalid, as Cecil was a minor. Monson claimed to be aware of this, but was determined to scam the insurance company anyway.

Bell and Littlejohn were brought in to perform an autopsy, where they drew the conclusion that Hambrough could not have killed himself, and that he was, in effect, murdered. A weapons test was performed by ballistics expert Dr. Patrick Heron Watson, who also confirmed Bell and Littlejohn's findings, stating that the shots were fired at a distance of around 10 feet, from someone actually standing behind the victim, which made a self-inflicted gunshot wound impossible. Imperative to this was a triangular wound they discovered on Hambrough's skull, which they deduced was made by cartridge fragments. Bell added that due to a lack of powder burns on Cecil's skull, and as a part of Cecil's skull was blown away, that the shot would have come from a distance of 10 feet; if Cecil had killed himself, there would've been only a 2-3 foot distance, which would have destroyed his skull. Over 100 witnesses were brought in to testify during Monson's trial.

The Crown (the British Monarchy) determined that Monson was a scam artist, and believed he was guilty of the murder, yet the judge instructed the jury not to use Monson's character as a determining element in achieving a verdict. Monson was acquitted, with a verdict of 'not proven', based on what the jury claimed was a lack of sufficient evidence. Bell later attributed to the verdict being the result of the judge being a novice.

When interviewed in the *Pall Mall Gazette* in 1893, Bell admitted that he had been called upon to serve the Crown in cases involving medical jurisprudence and handwriting analysis for over twenty years. He also mentioned his friendship with Littlejohn, who always requested Bell to accompany him on cases.

Even in his later life, Bell was still called upon to solve crimes, especially in terms of handwriting analysis. Though he respected the police and continued to work with them, Bell also grew somewhat frustrated, believing that the police weren't adequately trained to do their job, particularly in terms of observation and defining the facts of a case.

Bell and Pediatrics

As Bell was starting to get on in years, he remained active during his tenure as First Surgeon at the Royal Hospital for Sick Children, which began in 1887; there he confronted many childhood diseases, as well as worked with neglected and abused children, who were often being starved and beaten. As an advocate for children's rights, Bell's goal was to ensure that all children at the hospital be well taken care of and given much needed respect. Along these lines, he encouraged his nursing staff give the children exceptional care. He was tireless in his work, making sure the nurses received proper instruction on etiquette and sensitivity, so that they would be able to tend to the children properly. He strongly believed that nurses should be fully competent and have a complete understanding of the nature of their work.

Charity Work, Retirement and Honors

In his later years, Bell once again explored his literary aspirations. He flirted with writing poetry. Still greatly devastated by the death of his wife, even as the year's passed, his poetry resounded with his religious beliefs and gave him a productive outlet from which he could heal and grieve.

He had befriended Jessie M. Saxby, a well-respected author in her own right, who had penned numerous books of folklore and poetry based in the Shetland Islands. Saxby often asked Bell to proofread her fiction. She would later, in 1914, write an affectionate memoir about her platonic friendship with Bell, emphasizing that Bell devoted a great part of his time caring for the poor and unfortunate, as well as criminals.

Bell's religious devotion and belief that one should do God's work by helping others inspired him to give charitably to organizations like the Edinburgh Hospital for Incurables. His efforts earned him a visit from Queen Victoria to the Royal Infirmary of Edinburgh in 1881, where she greeted the patients in the Infirmary wards. Her Highness was a huge supporter of Bell's surgical methods and medical advances, and was greatly impressed by how he helped manage the diphtheria epidemic in 1864. The King of Siam also travelled to Scotland to visit the Royal Hospital for Sick Children in 1897; he would later send Bell congratulations on behalf of his fine work.

After an association of over 30 years and a member of its staff for 15 years, Bell resigned his position at the Royal Infirmary in 1886. He was given an emotional sendoff, with numerous accolades and praise from the staff and the students. The nursing staff, with the assistance of Florence Nightingale, presented Bell with elaborate gifts, including a writing desk, candelabras and an official portrait.

His departure from the Royal Infirmary didn't slow him down, nor did it actually completely take him away from the Royal Infirmary of Edinburgh. Shortly after resigning his position as Full Surgeon at the infirmary, he was asked to serve as the infirmary's Consulting Surgeon. He was also elected president to the Royal College of Surgeons of Edinburgh and appointed first surgeon at the Royal Hospital for Sick Children. It was this same year that his book, *Notes on Surgery for Nurses,* which he dedicated to Florence Nightingale, was published.

In 1891, Bell was honored by being elected President of the Medico-Chirurgical Society, a think tank for physicians, surgeons and general practitioners. In 1895, Bell was also chosen to be an assessor, in terms of education, for the University of Edinburgh, a position he held for the rest of his life.

Toward the end of the century, as Bell had been honored with new positions, he gradually resigned from some of his other posts which he had held for many years. In 1896, Bell retired from his post as Examiner for the Royal College of Surgeons, a position he held for 42 years, and he also said goodbye to his editorial stint as editor of the Edinburgh Medical Journal that same year. While he resigned as Chief Surgeon of the Royal Hospital for Sick Children in 1897, he stayed on board to serve as its Consulting Surgeon for the remainder of his life. With these new positions, Bell still remained an avid practitioner of medicine, making close to 20 house calls alone during the course of a day.

Bell also expressed a fascination with world events. As a young man he took interest in the developments of the American Civil War. Now he would eagerly read the newspapers to learn about ongoing events, such as the Dreyfus Affair and the Russo-Japanese War, while also expressing support for England's role in the Second Boer War (1899-1902), which defeated the Dutch-backed Orange Free State in South Africa. Interestingly enough, Doyle helped set up an army hospital in South Africa during the war and ardently supported the English cause, for which he was knighted.

According to one friend, Bell appeared liberal-minded, yet had conservative traits. He wasn't overtly political, but he often advocated for people to keep an open mind. Bell immersed himself in politics when Doyle was running for a parliament seat for the Liberal Union Party in 1900. The sad fact was that the campaign took an extremely nasty turn as Doyle's Catholic upbringing became fodder for his opponent, going even so much to slander him in political advertising. Bell spoke on behalf of Doyle, making it extremely clear that bigotry of any kind had no place in politics. All efforts were fruitless as Doyle eventually lost the campaign to Radical candidate G. M. Brown.

Toward the end of his life, Bell spent as much time with his grandchildren as possible. He enjoyed the company of children and animals, and had a plot of land set up at his country estate to serve as a burial ground for his pets. Bell was also an enthusiast of horse-drawn carriages, which led his grandchildren to affectionately refer to him as 'Gigs'. As horse drawn carriages were replaced by automobiles, Bell gave in and purchased a car in 1907. Uncomfortable driving the car himself, he hired a chauffeur, and once he grew accustomed to it, felt the efficiency of the automobile gave him greater accessibility to visit his patients and the hospitals he was associated with.

Bell died on October 4, 1911 at the age of 73. Coincidentally, the date signified his wife Edith's birthday. Bell's funeral was one of the largest in Edinburgh. It was well-attended by numerous members of the Edinburgh medical community, yet there appears to be no record of Doyle attending the funeral. One can only surmise that he was deeply affected by Bell's passing. Bell was mourned and praised for his work on behalf of the poor. One notable recollection involves a rather large man, who worked for the undertaker, sobbing uncontrollably into Bell's casket. Bell had treated this man's very ill son for years at no charge.

Talk of Bell's charity arose after his death. He privately helped fund several hospitals during his lifetime, and he bequeathed generous sums, at the time, to all of his servants, including his butler, his coachman and his gardener.

Chapter 7: Bell's Legacy

As a tribute to Bell's legacy, the Joseph Bell Centre for Forensic Statistics and Legal Reasoning was established at the University of Edinburgh in 2001. Using Bell as an example and an inspiration, the centre provides research, training and education in forensic statistics, while also incorporating elements of law and technology. The center teaches modern techniques on different kinds of reasoning, such as statistical, legal and facial recognition.

Bell's contribution to forensics, as well as his being the inspiration for Sherlock Holmes, have continued into the modern age, not just in terms of current television and movies, but also in terms of modern technology, such as computers.

As far back as 2003, software was being developed at the Bell Centre in Edinburgh, software that would allow detectives to investigate the differences between a death caused by a murder versus an accident or suicide. By using lateral thinking, the software was being touted as a tool that could also help prevent false arrests and imprisonment.

Apple Computers even devised a software application called Sherlock in 1998 that allowed users to search for files and web-related content. It provided the ability to surf the web, find local movie theaters and show times, as well as translate text into different languages. While popular among Apple users, the program was discontinued in 2007 in favor of new software.

By incorporating his knowledge of The Method and other medical techniques that he learned under Bell's tutelage, Doyle helped expand the public's consciousness on matters scientific. He had continued success as a writer, creating a vast array of mystery novels, historical novels and adventure tales that have been read for generations. He scored a major success with *The Lost World* (1912), an incredibly popular fantasy tale involving dinosaurs in the modern era, which has inspired several film, radio and television adaptations. He passed away at the age of 71 in 1930.

Sherlock Holmes has never gone out of style. Fan clubs and societies exist throughout the world honoring the importance of the beloved sleuth as well his creator, Sir Arthur Conan Doyle, and his inspiration, Joseph Bell. On the centennial of Bell's death in 2011, members of the official Japan Sherlock Holmes Club funded the erection of a plaque that was placed at the home where Bell spent his final years.

Conclusion

Bell was a forensic scientist, a pediatrician and an instructor, a man who pioneered not only forensic science, but the profession of nursing, clean surgical care, the modernization of sewage systems, and the treatment of neglected and abused children. In essence, Bell was actually one of the first supporters of women's rights.

Without Bell, we would likely not have any of the forensic science used in solving crimes today. We certainly wouldn't have one of history's most beloved literary characters, Sherlock Holmes. Bell's skills of observation and deduction extended far beyond their time, and are forever ingrained, not only in our practical applications, but in our imaginations.

Bibliography

Buczynski, Eric "Sherlock: The Forgotten Mac Application." Macinstruct, 29 March 2007. <http://www.macinstruct.com/node/88>

Calamai, Peter. The Real Sherlock Holmes. Cosmos Magazine 14 March 2008.

Cox, Michael. A Study in Celluloid: A Producer's Account of Jeremy Brett as Sherlock Holmes. Rupert Books, 1999.

Doyle, Sir Arthur Conan. The Complete Sherlock Holmes: All 4 Novels and 56 Short Stories. Bantam Classics.1986.

Edwards, Owen Dudley. "Doyle, Sir Arthur Ignatius Conan (1859–1930)." Oxford Dictionary of National Biography. Oxford University Press, 2004

Heifetz, Carl L. "Sherlock Holmes: The Education of the World's First Forensic Scientist." The Hounds Collection. Vol. 10, May 2005. 66-72.

Johnson, Roger. The District Messenger, The Newsletter of the Sherlock Holmes Society of London. 15 May 2007. no. 272

Liebow, Ely M. Dr. Joe Bell: Model for Sherlock Holmes. Popular Press, 1982.

Manners, Terry. The Man Who Became Sherlock Holmes - The Tortured Mind of Jeremy Brett. London: Virgin Publishing Ltd., 2001.

"NI Chemist Honours Sherlock Holmes." BBC News World Edition 16 October 2002. <http://news.bbc.co.uk/2/hi/uk_news/northern_irelan d/2332461.stm>

O'Brien, James. The Scientific Sherlock Holmes: Cracking the Case with Science and Forensics. Oxford University Press, 2013

"The Original 'Sherlock Holmes', An Interview with Dr. Joseph Bell." Pall Mall Gazette. 28 December 1893.

Raffensperger, John. "Was the real Sherlock Holmes a pediatric surgeon?" Journal of Pediatric Surgery (2010) 45, 1567-1570.

Ramsland, Katherine. "Observe Carefully, Deduce Shrewdly: Dr. Joseph Bell." The Forensic Examiner Fall 2009

"Sherlock Holmes software could solve crime cases." Pakistan Daily Times 11August 2003. <http://www.dailytimes.com.pk/default.asp?page=sto ry_11-8-2003_pg6_5>

Sherlock Holmes: The True Story. By Christopher Rowley. The Discovery Channel. 2003

Shreffler, Philip A., ed. <u>Sherlock Holmes by Gas Lamp: Highlights from the First Four Decades of the Baker Street Journal.</u> The Baker Street Irregulars, 1989.

Made in United States
Troutdale, OR
07/22/2023